delicious
desserts

THE AUSTRALIAN
Women's Weekly

CONTENTS

AUSTRALIAN CUP AND SPOON MEASUREMENTS ARE METRIC. A CONVERSION CHART APPEARS ON PAGE 77.

There's no denying it...dessert is the best part of the meal – it's what we didn't get as kids if we didn't finish our main meal. That was enough of a threat to get us to clean our plates. These desserts are worth finishing dinner for and, if you are lucky enough to have any left over the next day, they're just as good for an indulgent afternoon snack.

Pamela Clark

Food Director

BERRY CUSTARD FLAN

prep & cook time **45 minutes**
(+ refrigeration and cooling) serves **12**

1 cup (250ml) milk
¾ cup (180ml) pouring cream
1 vanilla bean
3 egg yolks
⅓ cup (75g) caster (superfine) sugar
¼ cup (35g) cornflour (cornstarch)
20g (¾ ounce) unsalted butter
500g (1 pound) mixed fresh berries
2 tablespoons raspberry jam,
    warmed, strained
1 tablespoon citrus-flavoured liqueur
pastry
1¼ cups (185g) plain (all-purpose) flour
¼ cup (55g) caster (superfine) sugar
125g (4 ounces) cold unsalted butter,
    chopped coarsely
1 egg yolk

1 Make pastry.
2 Roll pastry between sheets of baking paper until large enough to line 22cm (8¾ inch) round loose-based flan tin. Ease pastry into tin; press into side, trim edge. Prick base all over with fork. Cover, refrigerate 30 minutes.
3 Preheat oven to 200°C/400°F.
4 Place tin on oven tray. Line pastry case with baking paper; fill with dried beans or rice. Bake 12 minutes; remove paper and beans carefully from tin. Bake 5 minutes or until pastry is browned lightly; cool 15 minutes.
5 Meanwhile, combine milk and cream in small saucepan. Split vanilla bean in half, scrape seeds into pan; bring to the boil. Beat egg yolks, sugar and cornflour in small bowl with electric mixer until thick and creamy. Gradually beat hot milk mixture into egg mixture. Return mixture to pan; cook, stirring, until mixture boils and thickens. Stir in butter. Pour warm custard into pastry case; cover, refrigerate 3 hours.
6 Serve flan topped with berries; drizzle with combined jam and liqueur.
pastry Process flour, sugar and butter until crumbly. Add egg yolk; process until combined. Knead on floured surface until smooth. Wrap pastry in plastic; refrigerate 30 minutes.

notes **We used Cointreau in this recipe, but you can use any citrus-flavoured liqueur.**
The seeded vanilla pod can be pushed into a jar of caster sugar and used for baking. The pod will impart a vanilla flavour into the sugar.
Instead of using mixed fresh berries, use your favourite berry in the flan.

banana fritters

BANANA FRITTERS

prep & cook time **30 minutes** serves **4**

¼ cup (40g) icing (confectioners') sugar
2 teaspoons ground cinnamon
1 egg
¾ cup (50g) japanese breadcrumbs
vegetable oil, for deep-frying
4 large bananas (920g), halved lengthways

1 Combine icing sugar and cinnamon in a shallow medium bowl. Beat egg in a shallow medium bowl; place breadcrumbs in another shallow medium bowl.
2 Heat oil in medium saucepan.
3 Meanwhile, dip bananas in sugar mixture: shake off excess. Dip banana in egg, then in breadcrumbs to coat.
4 Deep-fry bananas, in batches, until browned. Drain on absorbent paper.
Serve with **ice-cream.**

note If you can't find japanese breadcrumbs, combine ½ cup stale white breadcrumbs and ¼ cup packaged breadcrumbs and use these instead; the taste and texture of the fritters won't be the same, however.

POACHED PEARS WITH CHOCOLATE SAUCE

prep & cook time **1 hour (+ cooling)** serves **4**

1.5 litres (6 cups) water
2 cups (500ml) port
½ cup (110g) caster (superfine) sugar
2 x 8cm (3 inch) strips orange rind
2 tablespoons orange juice
8 corella pears (480g), peeled
¼ cup (60ml) pouring cream
75g (2½ ounces) milk eating chocolate,
    chopped coarsely

poached pears with chocolate sauce

1 Combine the water, port, sugar, rind and juice in large saucepan. Add pears; bring to the boil. Reduce heat; simmer, covered, about 20 minutes or until pears are tender. Cool pears in syrup.
2 Remove pears from syrup; strain syrup into medium heatproof bowl. Return 2 cups of the strained syrup to same pan (discard remaining syrup); bring to the boil. Boil, uncovered, about 15 minutes or until syrup is reduced to about ½ cup; stir in cream, simmer until slightly thickened. Add chocolate, stir until smooth. Serve pears with chocolate sauce.

notes Corella pears are miniature dessert pears up to 10cm (4 inches) long; they are available from greengrocers. If you can't find corella pears, use four beurre bosc pears instead. Pears can be reheated gently in the syrup, or served cold. Sprinkle fine strips of orange rind over the pears to serve, if you like. The same quantity of red wine can be used in place of the port; the end result may not be as sweet, so adjust sweetening accordingly.

apple crumble

APPLE CRUMBLE

prep & cook time **50 minutes** serves **4**

5 large apples (1kg)
¼ cup (55g) caster (superfine) sugar
¼ cup (60ml) water
cinnamon crumble
½ cup (75g) self-raising flour
¼ cup (35g) plain (all-purpose) flour
½ cup (110g) firmly packed light brown sugar
100g (3½ ounces) cold butter, chopped
1 teaspoon ground cinnamon

1 Preheat oven to 180°C/350°F. Grease deep 1.5-litre (6-cup) baking dish.
2 Peel, core and quarter apples. Combine apple, sugar and the water in large saucepan; cook over low heat, covered, about 10 minutes. Drain; discard liquid.
3 Meanwhile, make crumble.
4 Place apple in dish; sprinkle with crumble. Bake about 25 minutes.
cinnamon crumble Blend or process ingredients until combined.

BANOFFEE PIE

prep & cook time **1 hour 20 minutes**
(+ refrigeration) serves **8**

395g (12¾ ounces) canned sweetened
condensed milk
75g (2½ ounces) butter, chopped
½ cup (110g) firmly packed light brown sugar
2 tablespoons golden syrup
2 large bananas (460g), sliced thinly
1¼ cups (310ml) thickened (heavy) cream,
whipped (see note)
pastry
1½ cups (225g) plain (all-purpose) flour
1 tablespoon icing (confectioners') sugar
140g (4½ ounces) cold butter, chopped
1 egg yolk
2 tablespoons cold water

1 Make pastry.
2 Grease 24cm (9½ inch) round loose-based fluted flan tin. Roll dough between sheets of baking paper until large enough to line tin. Ease dough into tin; press into base and side. Trim edge; prick base all over with fork. Cover; refrigerate 30 minutes.
3 Preheat oven to 200°C/400°F.
4 Place tin on oven tray. Line pastry case with baking paper; fill with dried beans or rice. Bake 10 minutes; remove paper and beans carefully from pie shell. Bake a further 10 minutes; cool.
5 Meanwhile, combine condensed milk, butter, sugar and syrup in medium saucepan; cook over medium heat, stirring, about 10 minutes or until mixture is caramel coloured. Stand 5 minutes; pour into pie shell, cool.
6 Top caramel with banana and whipped cream.
pastry Process flour, icing sugar and butter until crumbly; add egg yolk and water, process until ingredients come together. Knead dough on floured surface until smooth. Wrap in plastic wrap; refrigerate 30 minutes.

note **It is fine to use just 1 x 300ml carton of cream for this recipe.**

banoffee pie

LEMON MERINGUE PIE

prep & cook time **1 hour (+ refrigeration)** serves **10**

½ cup (75g) cornflour (cornstarch)
1 cup (220g) caster (superfine) sugar
½ cup (125ml) lemon juice
1¼ cups (310ml) water
2 teaspoons finely grated lemon rind
60g (2 ounces) unsalted butter, chopped
3 eggs, separated
½ cup (110g) caster (superfine) sugar, extra
pastry
1½ cups (225g) plain (all-purpose) flour
1 tablespoon icing (confectioners') sugar
140g (4½ ounces) cold butter, chopped
1 egg yolk
2 tablespoons cold water

1 Make pastry.
2 Grease 24cm (9½ inch) round loose-based fluted flan tin. Roll pastry between sheets of baking paper until large enough to line tin. Ease pastry into tin, press into base and side; trim edge. Cover; refrigerate 30 minutes.
3 Preheat oven to 240°C/475°F.
4 Place tin on oven tray. Line pastry case with baking paper; fill with dried beans or rice. Bake 15 minutes; remove paper and beans carefully from pie shell. Bake about 10 minutes; cool pie shell, turn oven off.
5 Meanwhile, combine cornflour and sugar in medium saucepan; gradually stir in juice and the water until smooth. Cook, stirring, over high heat, until mixture boils and thickens. Reduce heat; simmer, stirring, 1 minute. Remove from heat; stir in rind, butter and egg yolks. Cool 10 minutes.
6 Spread filling into pie shell. Cover; refrigerate 2 hours.
7 Preheat oven to 240°C/475°F.
8 Beat egg whites in small bowl with electric mixer until soft peaks form; gradually add extra sugar, beating until sugar dissolves.
9 Roughen surface of filling with fork before spreading with meringue mixture. Bake about 2 minutes or until meringue is browned lightly.
pastry Process flour, icing sugar and butter until crumbly. Add egg yolk and the water; process until ingredients come together. Knead dough on floured surface until smooth. Cover; refrigerate 30 minutes.

apple pie

APPLE PIE

prep & cook time **1 hour 45 minutes**
(+ refrigeration) serves 8

10 medium apples (1.5kg)
½ cup (125ml) water
¼ cup (55g) caster (superfine) sugar
1 teaspoon finely grated lemon rind
¼ teaspoon ground cinnamon
1 egg white
1 tablespoon caster (superfine) sugar, extra
pastry
1 cup (150g) plain (all-purpose) flour
½ cup (75g) self-raising flour
¼ cup (35g) cornflour (cornstarch)
¼ cup (30g) custard powder
1 tablespoon caster (superfine) sugar
100g (3½ ounces) cold butter,
   chopped coarsely
1 egg yolk
¼ cup (60ml) iced water

1 Make pastry.
2 Peel, core and slice apples thickly. Place apple and the water in large saucepan; bring to the boil. Reduce heat; simmer, covered, about 10 minutes or until apples soften. Drain; stir in sugar, rind and cinnamon. Cool.

3 Preheat oven to 220°C/425°F Grease deep 25cm (10 inch) pie dish.
4 Divide pastry in half. Roll one half between sheets of baking paper until large enough to line dish. Lift pastry into dish; press into base and side. Spoon apple mixture into pastry case; brush edge with egg white.
5 Roll remaining pastry large enough to cover filling; lift onto filling. Press edges together; trim away excess pastry. Brush pastry with egg white; sprinkle with extra sugar. Bake pie 20 minutes. Reduce oven temperature to 180°C/350°F; bake about 25 minutes or until golden brown.
pastry Process dry ingredients with the butter until crumbly. Add egg yolk and the water; process until combined. Knead on floured surface until smooth. Cover; refrigerate 30 minutes.
Serve with **vanilla custard or scoops of vanilla ice-cream.**

LEMON DELICIOUS PUDDINGS

prep & cook time **1 hour** serves 6

125g (4 ounces) butter, melted
2 teaspoons finely grated lemon rind
1½ cups (330g) caster (superfine) sugar
3 eggs, separated
½ cup (75g) self-raising flour
⅓ cup (80ml) lemon juice
1⅓ cups (330ml) milk

1 Preheat oven to 180°C/350°F Grease six 1-cup (250ml) ovenproof dishes; place in large baking dish.
2 Combine butter, rind, sugar and yolks in large bowl. Whisk in sifted flour then juice. Gradually whisk in milk; mixture should be smooth and runny.
3 Beat egg whites in small bowl with electric mixer until soft peaks form; fold into lemon mixture in two batches.
4 Divide lemon mixture among dishes. Add enough boiling water to baking dish to come halfway up side of ovenproof dishes. Bake about 30 minutes or until puddings have risen and are a light golden colour.

lemon delicious puddings

BLACK FOREST TRIFLE

prep & cook time **50 minutes (+ refrigeration)** serves **10**

440g (14 ounces) canned seeded
   black cherries in syrup
345g (11 ounces) frozen chocolate cake
¼ cup (60ml) cherry brandy
2 teaspoons cocoa powder
chocolate custard
5 egg yolks
½ cup (110g) caster (superfine) sugar
1 cup (250ml) milk
¾ cup (180ml) pouring cream
100g (3½ ounces) dark (semi-sweet) eating
   chocolate, chopped coarsely
mascarpone cream
1¼ cups (310ml) pouring cream
1 cup (250g) mascarpone cheese
2 teaspoons vanilla extract
¼ cup (40g) icing (confectioners') sugar
chocolate curls
100g (3½ ounces) dark (semi-sweet)
   chocolate Melts

1 Make chocolate custard.
2 Make mascarpone cream.
3 Drain cherries; reserve ¼ cup of the syrup.
4 Discard any icing from chocolate cake. Coarsely chop cake; place in deep 3-litre (12-cup) serving bowl. Sprinkle cake with cherries and combined brandy and reserved syrup. Top with chocolate custard and mascarpone cream. Cover; refrigerate 3 hours or overnight.
5 Make chocolate curls.
6 Top trifle with chocolate curls and sifted cocoa powder.

chocolate custard Whisk egg yolks and sugar in medium bowl until combined. Combine milk, cream and chocolate in medium saucepan; stir over low heat until mixture comes to the boil; remove from heat. Gradually whisk hot chocolate mixture into yolk mixture. Return mixture to pan; stir over low heat, without boiling, about 10 minutes or until mixture is slightly thickened and coats the back of a spoon. Cover custard; refrigerate until chilled.

mascarpone cream Beat ingredients in small bowl with electric mixer until soft peaks form. Cover; refrigerate until chilled.

chocolate curls Place chocolate in small heatproof bowl; using wooden spoon, stir chocolate over small saucepan of simmering water until smooth. Spread chocolate evenly over marble or a foil-covered surface. When chocolate is almost set, drag ice-cream scoop over surface of chocolate to make curls.

note **The chocolate custard can be made a day ahead.**

chocolate mousse

CHOCOLATE MOUSSE

prep & cook time **35 minutes (+ refrigeration)** serves 6

**200g (6½ ounces) dark (semi-sweet) eating
chocolate, chopped coarsely**
30g (1 ounce) unsalted butter
3 eggs, separated (see notes)
**1¼ cups (310ml) thickened (heavy) cream,
whipped (see notes)**

1 Melt chocolate and butter in large heatproof
glass bowl over large saucepan of simmering
water (do not allow water to touch base of bowl).
Remove from heat. Stir in egg yolks; cool.
2 Beat egg whites in small bowl with electric
mixer until soft peaks form.
3 Fold cream into chocolate mixture then fold
in egg whites, in two batches.
4 Divide mousse into serving dishes; refrigerate
3 hours or overnight.
Serve with **whipped cream and chocolate curls.**

notes **The eggs must be at room temperature for
success with this recipe.**
It's fine to use just 1 x 300ml carton of cream.

PECAN PIE

prep & cook time **1 hour 25 minutes**
(+ refrigeration) serves **10**

1 cup (120g) pecans, chopped coarsely
2 tablespoons cornflour (cornstarch)
1 cup (220g) firmly packed light brown sugar
60g (2 ounces) butter, melted
2 tablespoons pouring cream
1 teaspoon vanilla extract
3 eggs
⅓ cup (40g) pecans, extra
2 tablespoons apricot jam, warmed, sieved
pastry
1¼ cups (185g) plain (all-purpose) flour
⅓ cup (55g) icing (confectioners') sugar
125g (4 ounces) cold butter, chopped
1 egg yolk
1 teaspoon water

1 Make pastry.
2 Grease 24cm (9½ inch) round loose-based
flan tin. Roll pastry between sheets of baking
paper until large enough to line tin. Ease pastry
into tin, press into base and side; trim edge.
Cover; refrigerate 30 minutes.
3 Preheat oven to 180°C/350°F.
4 Place tin on oven tray. Line pastry case with
baking paper, fill with dried beans or rice. Bake
10 minutes; remove paper and beans carefully
from pie shell. Bake about 5 minutes; cool.
5 Reduce oven temperature to 160°C/325°F.
6 Combine chopped nuts and cornflour in
medium bowl. Add sugar, butter, cream, extract
and eggs; stir until combined. Pour mixture into
shell, sprinkle with extra nuts.
7 Bake about 45 minutes. Cool; brush pie
with jam.
pastry Process flour, icing sugar and butter
until crumbly. Add egg yolk and the water;
process until ingredients just come together.
Knead dough on floured surface until smooth.
Cover; refrigerate 30 minutes.

pecan pie

PAVLOVA SHELLS

PAVLOVA TRIFLES

prep time **25 minutes** serves **4**

Beat ¾ cup thickened (heavy) cream and
2 tablespoons icing (confectioners') sugar in
small bowl with electric mixer until soft peaks
form; stir in 200g (6½ ounces) crème fraîche.
Divide 250g (8 ounces) quartered strawberries
and 2 thickly sliced medium bananas among
four 1½-cup (375ml) glasses. Top with ¼ cup
passionfruit pulp. Divide crème fraîche mixture
into glasses; top with 45g (1½ ounces) coarsely
chopped mini pavlova shells, 3 coarsely chopped
kiwifruit and another ¼ cup passionfruit pulp.

notes You need 6 passionfruit to get the required
amount of pulp for this recipe.
Packaged pavlova shells (also called cases or nests)
can be found at supermarkets.

STRAWBERRY MERINGUE CREAM

prep time **15 minutes** serves **6**

Combine 500g (1 pound) quartered strawberries
and 1 tablespoon orange-flavoured liqueur
in medium bowl. Beat 1¼ cups thickened
(heavy) cream and 2 tablespoons icing sugar
(confectioners' sugar) in small bowl with electric
mixer until soft peaks form. Fold in ½ cup yogurt.
Place half of the strawberries in 1.25-litre
(5-cup) serving dish. Top with 45g (1½ ounces)
coarsely chopped mini pavlova shells and half
of the cream mixture. Repeat layering with
remaining strawberries, cream mixture and
another 45g (1½ ounces) coarsely chopped
mini pavlova shells.

note It's fine to use just 1 x 300ml carton of cream.

BANANA MERINGUE SUNDAE

prep time **15 minutes** serves **4**

Beat 1¼ cups thickened (heavy) cream and
2 tablespoons lemon-flavoured spread in small
bowl with electric mixer until soft peaks form.
Layer lemon cream, 45g (1½ ounces) coarsely
chopped mini pavlova shells, ½ cup passionfruit
pulp and 4 coarsely chopped small bananas
among serving glasses.

notes **You need 6 passionfruit to get the required
amount of pulp for this recipe.
It's fine to use just 1 x 300ml carton of cream.**

LEMON MERINGUE SUNDAE

prep & cook time **10 minutes** serves **4**

Stir ⅔ cup lemon butter and ⅓ cup pouring
cream in small saucepan, over low heat, until
smooth; cool 10 minutes. Layer 1 litre (4 cups)
ice-cream, lemon butter mixture and 45g
(1½ ounces) coarsely chopped mini pavlova
shells in four serving glasses.

marshmallow pavlova

meringue top will fall on top of the marshmallow centre). Serve pavlova topped with whipped cream, strawberries and passionfruit.

note It's fine to use just 1 x 300ml carton of cream.

MARSHMALLOW PAVLOVA

prep & cook time 1 hour 50 minutes (+ cooling) serves 8

4 egg whites
1 cup (220g) caster (superfine) sugar
½ teaspoon vanilla extract
¾ teaspoon white vinegar
1¼ cups (310ml) thickened (heavy) cream, whipped (see note)
250g (8 ounces) strawberries, halved
¼ cup (60ml) passionfruit pulp

1 Preheat oven to 120°C/250°F. Line oven tray with foil; grease foil, dust with cornflour, shake away excess. Mark 18cm (7 inch) circle on foil.
2 Beat egg whites in small bowl with electric mixer until soft peaks form; gradually add sugar, beating until sugar dissolves. Add extract and vinegar; beat until combined.
3 Spread meringue into circle on foil, building up at the side to 8cm (3 inches) in height. Smooth side and top of pavlova gently. Using spatula blade, mark decorative grooves around side of pavlova; smooth top again.
4 Bake pavlova about 1½ hours. Turn oven off; cool pavlova in oven with door ajar.
5 Cut around top edge of pavlova (the crisp

TOFFEE, DATE AND GINGER PUDDINGS

prep & cook time 1 hour makes 6

½ cup (115g) finely chopped glacé ginger
½ cup (60g) finely chopped roasted walnuts
1 cup (140g) seeded dried dates
¾ cup (180ml) water
1 teaspoon bicarbonate of soda (baking soda)
45g (1½ ounces) butter, chopped coarsely
½ cup (110g) firmly packed light brown sugar
2 eggs
¾ cup (110g) self-raising flour
1 teaspoon ground ginger
ginger butterscotch sauce
½ cup (110g) firmly packed light brown sugar
⅔ cup (160ml) pouring cream
100g (3½ ounces) butter, chopped coarsely
½ teaspoon ground ginger

1 Preheat oven to 160°C/325°F. Grease six-hole ¾-cup (180ml) texas muffin pan; line bases with small rounds of baking paper.
2 Combine glacé ginger and nuts in small bowl; sprinkle mixture over pan holes.
3 Combine dates and the water in small saucepan; bring to the boil. Remove from heat; stir in soda. Stand 5 minutes.
4 Blend or process date mixture with butter and sugar until smooth. Add eggs, flour and ground ginger; process until combined.
5 Pour mixture into pan holes; bake about 30 minutes. Stand 5 minutes; turn onto wire rack to cool 5 minutes.
6 Meanwhile, make ginger butterscotch sauce.
7 Serve warm puddings drizzled with sauce.
ginger butterscotch sauce Stir ingredients in small saucepan over low heat until smooth. Simmer, uncovered, 5 minutes.

note Be careful when measuring the bicarbonate of soda; too much will cause a bitter flavour in the pudding.

toffee, date and ginger puddings

APPLE TARTE TARTIN

prep & cook time **1 hour 20 minutes**
(+ standing) serves **8**

6 medium golden delicious apples (900g)
2 tablespoons lemon juice
4 sheets ready-rolled puff pastry
1 cup (220g) caster (superfine) sugar
100g (3½ ounces) unsalted butter,
**   chopped coarsely**
¼ cup (60ml) water

1 Preheat oven to 200°C/400°F.
2 Peel, core and quarter apples; combine with juice in medium bowl.
3 Brush two pastry sheets with water; top with remaining sheets, press firmly together. Cut an 18cm (7 inch) round from both pastry sheets.
4 Combine sugar, butter and the water in medium frying pan; stir over heat until sugar dissolves. Bring to the boil; reduce heat, simmer, without stirring, about 15 minutes, shaking pan occasionally, until dark caramel in colour. Allow bubbles to subside. Carefully pour caramel into two shallow 16cm (6¼ inch) round fluted metal pie tins. Add ¼ cup water to the hot frying pan; stir to mix with any caramel remaining in pan. Reserve caramel mixture.

5 Position apple quarters in tins. Cut any remaining apple in half and place in tins to fill in any gaps.
6 Brush apple with reserved caramel; cover tarts with foil, bake 15 minutes.
7 Remove foil from tarts; carefully top apples with pastry rounds, tuck pastry down between the side of the tin and the apples. Bake about 30 minutes or until pastry is golden brown.
8 Stand 1 hour before turning onto serving plate.

notes **It's important to pack as many pieces of apple into the tins as possible as they shrink during cooking. Golden delicious apples are the best for this recipe, but granny smith will do the job, too.**
The pie is at its best after it's been removed from the oven for 1 hour. Instead of making two smaller tarte tartins you could make one larger one. If doing so, reduce the pastry sheets to two and cut into 23cm (9 inch) rounds; use a 22cm (8¾ inch) round metal pie tin.

date and butterscotch self-saucing pudding

WHITE CHOCOLATE AND RASPBERRY CROISSANT PUDDING
prep & cook time **1 hour 15 minutes** serves **8**

5 croissants (300g), sliced thinly
⅓ cup (110g) raspberry jam
100g (3½ ounces) white eating chocolate, chopped coarsely
1 cup (135g) raspberries
custard
1½ cups (375ml) pouring cream
1¼ cups (310ml) milk
⅓ cup (75g) caster (superfine) sugar
1 teaspoon vanilla extract
4 eggs

1 Preheat oven to 160°C/325°F.
2 Make custard.
3 Grease shallow 2-litre (8-cup) ovenproof dish. Layer croissant slices, overlapping slightly, in dish; dollop spoonfuls of jam over slices. Sprinkle with chocolate and berries. Pour custard over the top; stand 5 minutes.
4 Place dish in large baking dish; add enough boiling water to come halfway up sides of ovenproof dish. Bake about 1 hour or until pudding sets. Remove pudding from baking dish; stand 5 minutes before serving.
custard Combine cream, milk, sugar and extract in medium saucepan; bring to the boil. Whisk eggs in large bowl; whisking constantly, gradually add hot milk mixture to egg mixture.

notes Any type of berries, fresh or frozen, can be used instead of the raspberries in this pudding.
If you prefer, use dark (semi-sweet) or milk eating chocolate in place of the white chocolate.
Sprinkle the pudding with sifted icing (confectioners') sugar and serve with a good quality ice-cream for a truly indulgent dessert.

DATE AND BUTTERSCOTCH SELF-SAUCING PUDDING
prep & cook time **1 hour** serves **6**

1 cup (150g) self-raising flour
½ cup (110g) firmly packed light brown sugar
20g (¾ ounce) butter, melted
½ cup (125ml) milk
½ cup (70g) finely chopped dried seedless dates
caramel sauce
½ cup (110g) firmly packed light brown sugar
1¾ cups (430ml) boiling water
45g (1½ ounces) butter

1 Preheat oven to 180°C/350°F. Grease 2-litre (8-cup) shallow ovenproof dish.
2 Combine flour, sugar, butter, milk and dates in medium bowl. Spread mixture into dish.
3 Make caramel sauce.
4 Pour caramel sauce slowly over the back of a spoon onto mixture in dish. Bake about 45 minutes or until centre is firm. Stand 5 minutes before serving.
caramel sauce Combine ingredients in medium heatproof jug; stir until sugar is dissolved.

white chocolate and raspberry croissant pudding

chocolate hazelnut torte

CHOCOLATE HAZELNUT TORTE

prep & cook time **1 hour** serves **10**

5 egg whites
1¼ cups (275g) caster (superfine) sugar
1½ cups (150g) ground hazelnuts
1 cup (320g) chocolate hazelnut spread
2½ cups (625ml) thickened (heavy) cream,
    whipped
2 teaspoons cocoa powder

1 Preheat oven to 160°C/325°F. Line two large oven trays with baking paper. Using a pencil, mark two 12cm x 25cm (4¾ inch x 10 inch) rectangles on each tray. Turn paper over so that the pencil marks are facing down.
2 Beat egg whites in medium bowl with electric mixer until soft peaks form. Gradually add sugar, beating until dissolved. Fold in ground hazelnuts.
3 Spread one quarter of the mixture evenly over each outlined rectangle. Bake, swapping trays halfway through baking, about 40 minutes or until crisp. Cool on trays.
4 Place the chocolate hazelnut spread in small microwave-safe bowl. Microwave on HIGH (100%) for 20 seconds or until of a soft, spreadable consistency. Spread three of the meringue rectangles evenly with the chocolate hazelnut spread; reserve the remaining meringue rectangle for the top layer.
5 Place one of the chocolate-topped meringue rectangles on a serving plate. Spread with one third of the whipped cream. Continue layering with remaining chocolate-topped meringue rectangles and cream. Top with the remaining plain meringue rectangle. Serve dusted with sifted cocoa.

chocolate self-saucing pudding

CHOCOLATE SELF-SAUCING PUDDING

prep & cook time **50 minutes** serves **6**

1 cup (150g) self-raising flour
½ teaspoon bicarbonate of soda (baking soda)
½ cup (50g) cocoa powder
1¼ cups (275g) firmly packed light brown sugar
75g (2½ ounces) butter, melted
½ cup (120g) sour cream
1 egg
2 cups (500ml) boiling water

1 Preheat oven to 180°C/350°F. Grease deep 1.5-litre (6-cup) ovenproof dish.
2 Sift flour, soda, half of the cocoa and ½ cup of the sugar into medium bowl; stir in combined butter, sour cream and egg.
3 Spread mixture into dish. Sift remaining cocoa and remaining sugar evenly over mixture; gently pour over the boiling water. Bake pudding about 40 minutes. Stand 5 minutes before serving.
Serve with **vanilla ice-cream.**

CHOCOLATE RASPBERRY TART

prep & cook time **45 minutes (+ refrigeration)** serves **12**

¾ cup (240g) raspberry jam
200g (6½ ounces) dark (semi-sweet) eating
   chocolate, chopped finely
30g (1 ounce) unsalted butter, melted
⅔ cup (160ml) pouring cream, warmed
125g (4 ounces) raspberries
pastry
1¼ cups (185g) plain (all-purpose) flour
½ cup (80g) icing (confectioners') sugar
125g (4 ounces) cold unsalted butter,
   chopped coarsely
¼ cup (60ml) iced water, approximately

1 Make pastry.
2 Grease 12cm x 35cm (4¾ inch x 14 inch)
(or 24cm/9½ inch round) loose-based flan tin.
Roll pastry between sheets of baking paper
until large enough to line tin. Ease pastry into
tin, press into base and sides; trim edge, prick
base with fork. Cover; refrigerate 30 minutes.
3 Preheat oven to 200°C/400°F.
4 Place tin on oven tray; cover pastry case with
baking paper, fill with dried beans or uncooked
rice. Bake 15 minutes; remove paper and
beans carefully from pastry case. Bake about
10 minutes. Spread jam over pastry base;
return to oven for 2 minutes. Cool.
5 Combine chocolate, butter and cream in
medium bowl; whisk until smooth. Pour chocolate
mixture into pastry case; refrigerate 2 hours.
Top tart with raspberries.
pastry Process flour, icing sugar and butter
until crumbly; add enough of the water to make
ingredients come together. Knead dough gently
on floured surface until smooth. Wrap in plastic
wrap; refrigerate 30 minutes.

warm chocolate pavlovas

WARM CHOCOLATE PAVLOVAS

prep & cook time **40 minutes** serves **4**

2 egg whites
1⅓ cups (215g) icing (confectioners') sugar
⅓ cup (80ml) boiling water
1 tablespoon cocoa powder, sifted
2 cups (500ml) chocolate ice-cream
chocolate custard sauce
1 tablespoon cornflour (cornstarch)
1 tablespoon cocoa powder, sifted
1 tablespoon caster (superfine) sugar
1 cup (125ml) milk
2 egg yolks

1 Preheat oven to 180°C/350°F. Line large oven tray with baking paper.
2 Beat egg whites, icing sugar and the water in small bowl with electric mixer about 10 minutes or until firm peaks form.
3 Fold sifted cocoa into meringue. Drop six equal amounts of mixture onto tray; use the back of a spoon to create well in centre of mounds. Bake about 25 minutes or until firm to touch.
4 Meanwhile, make chocolate custard sauce.
5 Serve pavlovas straight from the oven, topped with sauce and ice-cream.
chocolate custard sauce Blend cornflour cocoa and sugar with milk in small saucepan. Stir in egg yolks. Stir over heat until sauce boils and thickens.

CRÊPES SUZETTE

prep & cook time **1 hour 40 minutes (+ standing)** serves **4**

¾ cup (110g) plain (all-purpose) flour
3 eggs
2 tablespoons vegetable oil
¾ cup (180ml) milk
orange sauce
125g (4 ounces) unsalted butter
½ cup (110g) caster (superfine) sugar
1½ cups (375ml) orange juice
2 tablespoons lemon juice
⅓ cup (80ml) orange-flavoured liqueur

crêpes suzette

1 Sift flour into medium bowl, make well in centre; add eggs and oil then gradually whisk in milk until smooth. Pour batter into large jug, cover; stand 1 hour.
2 Heat greased heavy-based crêpe pan or small frying pan; pour ¼ cup of batter into pan, tilting pan to coat base. Cook, over low heat, until browned lightly, loosening edge of crêpe with spatula. Turn crêpe; brown other side. Remove crêpe from pan; cover to keep warm. Repeat with remaining batter to make a total of 8 crêpes, greasing pan each time.
3 Make orange sauce. Fold crêpes in half then in half again, place in sauce; warm over low heat.
4 Remove crêpes to serving plates; pour hot sauce over crêpes. Serve with orange segments, if you like.
orange sauce Melt butter in large frying pan, add sugar; cook, stirring, until mixture begins to brown. Add strained juices; bring to the boil. Reduce heat; simmer, uncovered, about 3 minutes or until a golden colour. Remove from heat; add liqueur, ignite.

note **Be careful when igniting the sauce – turn off overhead exhaust fans. Igniting the sauce burns off the alcohol, leaving a more intense flavour, however, the sauce can be served as is, without first igniting it.**

steamed ginger pudding

maintain level. Stand pudding 5 minutes before turning onto plate.

5 Meanwhile, make syrup.

6 Serve pudding topped with syrup.

syrup Stir ingredients in small saucepan over heat until smooth; bring to the boil. Reduce heat; simmer, uncovered, 2 minutes.

SOFT-CENTRED MOCHA PUDDINGS

prep & cook time **40 minutes** makes **6**

155g (5 ounces) dark (semi-sweet) eating
   chocolate, chopped coarsely
125g (4 ounces) butter, chopped coarsely
3 teaspoons instant coffee granules
2 eggs
2 egg yolks
⅓ cup (75g) caster (superfine) sugar
¼ cup (35g) plain (all-purpose) flour
2 teaspoons cocoa powder

1 Preheat oven to 200°C/400°F. Grease six-hole (¾-cup/180ml) texas muffin pan well with softened butter.

2 Stir chocolate, butter and coffee in small saucepan, over low heat, until smooth; cool 10 minutes. Transfer to large bowl.

3 Beat eggs, egg yolks and sugar in small bowl with electric mixer until thick and creamy. Fold egg mixture and sifted flour into barely warm chocolate mixture.

4 Divide mixture among pan holes; bake about 12 minutes.

5 Gently turn puddings onto serving plates, top-side down. Serve immediately, dusted with sifted cocoa powder.

Serve with whipped cream and fresh raspberries.

note Use a good-quality dark chocolate with 70% cocoa solids.

STEAMED GINGER PUDDING

prep & cook time **1 hour 15 minutes** serves **6**

60g (2 ounces) butter
¼ cup (90g) golden syrup
½ teaspoon bicarbonate of soda (baking soda)
1 cup (150g) self-raising flour
2 teaspoons ground ginger
½ cup (125ml) milk
1 egg
syrup
⅓ cup (115g) golden syrup
2 tablespoons water
30g (1 ounce) butter

1 Grease 1.25-litre (5-cup) pudding steamer.

2 Combine butter and syrup in small saucepan; stir over low heat until smooth. Remove from heat, stir in soda; transfer mixture to medium bowl. Stir in sifted dry ingredients then combined milk and egg, in two batches.

3 Spread mixture into steamer. Cover with pleated baking paper and foil; secure with lid.

4 Place pudding steamer in large saucepan with enough boiling water to come halfway up side of steamer; cover pan with tight-fitting lid. Boil 1 hour, replenishing water as necessary to

soft-centred mocha puddings

bread and butter pudding

BREAD AND BUTTER PUDDING

prep & cook time **1 hour 15 minutes** serves **6**

6 slices white bread (270g)
45g (1½ ounces) butter, softened
½ cup (80g) sultanas
¼ teaspoon ground nutmeg
custard
1½ cups (375ml) milk
2 cups (500ml) pouring cream
⅓ cup (75g) caster (superfine) sugar
1 teaspoon vanilla extract
4 eggs

1 Preheat oven to 160°C/325°F. Grease shallow 2-litre (8-cup) ovenproof dish.
2 Make custard.
3 Trim crusts from bread. Spread each slice with butter; cut into four triangles. Layer bread, overlapping, in dish; sprinkle with sultanas. Pour custard over bread; sprinkle with nutmeg. Stand 5 minutes.
4 Place ovenproof dish in large baking dish; add enough boiling water to come halfway up side of ovenproof dish. Bake about 45 minutes or until pudding is set. Remove pudding from baking dish; stand 5 minutes before serving. Serve dusted with sifted icing (confectioners') sugar, if you like.
custard Combine milk, cream, sugar and extract in medium saucepan; bring to the boil. Whisk eggs in large bowl; whisking constantly, gradually add hot milk mixture to egg mixture.

chocolate soufflés

CHOCOLATE SOUFFLÉS

prep & cook time **35 minutes** serves **4**

⅓ cup (75g) caster (superfine) sugar
45g (1½ ounces) butter
1 tablespoon plain (all-purpose) flour
200g (6½ ounces) dark (semi-sweet)
    eating chocolate, melted
2 egg yolks
4 egg whites

1 Preheat oven to 180°C/350°F. Grease four ¾-cup (180ml) soufflé dishes. Sprinkle inside of dishes with a little of the sugar; shake away excess. Place dishes on oven tray.
2 Melt butter in small saucepan, add flour; cook, stirring, about 2 minutes or until mixture thickens and bubbles. Remove from heat; stir in chocolate and egg yolks. Transfer to large bowl.
3 Beat egg whites in small bowl with electric mixer until soft peaks form. Gradually add remaining sugar, beating until sugar dissolves. Fold egg white mixture into chocolate mixture, in two batches.
4 Divide soufflé mixture among dishes; bake about 15 minutes. Dust with sifted cocoa powder, if desired.

POACHED PEARS AND QUINCE WITH ALMOND CRUMBLE

prep & cook time **2 hours 30 minutes** serves **6**

3 cups (660g) caster (superfine) sugar
3 cups (750ml) water
3 medium quinces (1kg), peeled, quartered,
   cored
2 strips lemon rind
3 medium pears (700g), peeled, halved, cored
2 tablespoons lemon juice, approximately
almond crumble
½ cup (75g) plain (all-purpose) flour
75g (2½ ounces) butter, chopped
⅓ cup (75g) firmly packed light brown sugar
1 teaspoon ground cinnamon
½ cup (80g) coarsely chopped almond kernels

1 Combine sugar and the water in large saucepan; stir over low heat until sugar dissolves. Add quinces and rind; bring to the boil. Reduce heat; simmer, covered, about 1¾ hous or until quince is tender and rosy pink.
2 Meanwhile, make almond crumble.
3 Remove quince from syrup with slotted spoon. Add pear to same syrup; bring to the boil. Reduce heat, simmer, uncovered, about 10 minutes or until pears are tender. Remove with slotted spoon.
4 Boil syrup, uncovered, until reduced to 2 cups. Adjust the sweetness of the syrup with juice to taste.
5 Spoon a little syrup over the fruit. Sprinkle fruit with almond crumble.
almond crumble Preheat oven to 160°C/325°F. Sift flour into medium bowl; rub in butter. Add sugar, cinnamon and almonds; mix well. Place mixture on oven tray; bake about 30 minutes or until browned and crisp, turning occasionally with an egg slicer to retain large pieces.
Serve with custard, cream or ice-cream.

note Recipe can be prepared several hours ahead. Reheat the fruit in the syrup before serving.

passionfruit soufflés

PASSIONFRUIT SOUFFLÉS

prep & cook time **25 minutes** makes **4**

15g (½ ounce) butter, softened
1 tablespoon caster (superfine) sugar
2 eggs, separated
155g (5 ounces) canned passionfruit in syrup
⅔ cup (110g) icing (confectioners') sugar
4 egg whites
1 tablespoon icing (confectioners') sugar,
  extra

1 Preheat oven to 220°C/425°F. Grease four
1-cup (250ml) soufflé dishes with butter; sprinkle
with caster sugar, shake away excess.
2 Combine egg yolks, passionfruit and half the
sifted icing sugar in large bowl.
3 Beat all the egg whites in a small bowl with
electric mixer until soft peaks form; add remaining
sifted icing sugar, beat until firm peaks form.
Gently fold a third of the egg white mixture into
passionfruit mixture, then fold in remaining egg
white mixture.
4 Place dishes on oven tray. Spoon soufflé
mixture into dishes; bake about 12 minutes or
until soufflés are puffed and golden. Dust with
extra sifted icing sugar; serve immediately.

TIRAMISU

prep time **30 minutes** (+ refrigeration) serves **8**

2 tablespoons ground espresso coffee
1 cup (250ml) boiling water
½ cup (125ml) marsala
250g (8 ounces) sponge finger biscuits
1¼ cups (310ml) thickened (heavy) cream
  (see notes)
¼ cup (40g) icing (confectioners') sugar
2 cups (500g) mascarpone cheese
2 tablespoons marsala, extra
2 teaspoons cocoa powder

tiramisu

1 Combine coffee and the water in coffee
plunger; stand 2 minutes before plunging.
Combine coffee mixture and marsala in
medium heatproof bowl; cool 10 minutes.
2 Place half the biscuits, in single layer, over
base of deep 2-litre (8-cup) dish; drizzle with
half the coffee mixture.
3 Beat cream and sifted icing sugar in small
bowl with electric mixer until soft peaks form;
transfer to large bowl. Fold in combined
mascarpone cheese and extra marsala.
4 Spread half the cream mixture over biscuits
in dish. Submerge the remaining biscuits, one
at a time, in coffee mixture, taking care the
biscuits do not become so soggy that they fall
apart; place over cream layer. Top biscuit layer
with the remaining cream mixture. Cover;
refrigerate 3 hours or overnight.
5 Serve tiramisu dusted with sifted cocoa.

notes It's fine to use just 1 x 300ml carton of cream.
Sponge finger biscuits are also known as savoy or
savoiardi biscuits, lady's fingers or sponge fingers; they
are Italian-style crisp fingers made from sponge-cake
mixture, and are available from most supermarkets.

rice pudding

CHOCOLATE PISTACHIO PUDDINGS WITH CHOCOLATE FUDGE SAUCE

prep & cook time **50 minutes** makes **6**

½ cup (70g) coarsely chopped pistachios
125g (4 ounces) butter, softened
2 teaspoons vanilla extract
1 cup (220g) caster (superfine) sugar
2 eggs
²/₃ cup (100g) self-raising flour
¹/₃ cup (35g) cocoa powder
¹/₃ cup (25g) stale breadcrumbs
¹/₃ cup (80ml) milk
¹/₃ cup (60g) coarsely grated dark
    (semi-sweet) eating chocolate
chocolate fudge sauce
155g (5 ounces) dark (semi-sweet) eating
    chocolate, chopped coarsely
20g (¾ ounce) butter
²/₃ cup (160ml) pouring cream

1 Preheat oven to 180°C/350°F. Grease six 1-cup (250ml) dariole moulds.
2 Sprinkle nuts evenly over the base of each mould; place on oven tray.
3 Beat butter, extract and sugar in medium bowl with electric mixer until just combined. Add eggs, one at a time. Stir in sifted flour and cocoa, then breadcrumbs, milk and chocolate. Spoon mixture into the moulds. Bake about 30 minutes. Stand 5 minutes before turning, top-side down, onto serving plates.
4 Meanwhile, make chocolate fudge sauce.
5 Serve puddings with chocolate fudge sauce, sprinkled with extra pistachios and thick (heavy) cream, if desired.
chocolate fudge sauce Place chocolate and butter in medium heatproof bowl over medium saucepan of simmering water (do not allow water to touch the base of the bowl). Stir until mixture is smooth; stir in cream.

note Recipe can be made several hours ahead. Reheat puddings briefly in the microwave just before serving. Chocolate fudge sauce best made just before serving.

RICE PUDDING

prep & cook time **1 hour 30 minutes** serves **6**

½ cup (100g) uncooked white
    medium-grain rice
2½ cups (625ml) milk
¼ cup (55g) caster (superfine) sugar
¼ cup (40g) sultanas
½ teaspoon vanilla extract
2 teaspoons butter
½ teaspoon ground nutmeg

1 Preheat oven to 160°C/325°F. Grease shallow 1-litre (4-cup) baking dish.
2 Wash rice under cold water; drain well. Combine rice, milk, sugar, sultanas and extract in dish; whisk lightly with fork. Dot with butter.
3 Bake 1 hour, whisking lightly with fork under skin occasionally. Sprinkle with nutmeg; bake a further 20 minutes. Serve warm or cold.

chocolate pistachio puddings with chocolate fudge sauce

CRÈME CARAMEL

prep & cook time **1 hour (+ refrigeration)** serves **6**

¾ cup (165g) caster (superfine) sugar
½ cup (125ml) water
1¼ cups (310ml) pouring cream (see note)
1¾ cups (430ml) milk
6 eggs
1 teaspoon vanilla extract
⅓ cup (75g) caster (superfine) sugar, extra

1 Preheat oven to 160°C/325°F.
2 Combine sugar and the water in medium frying pan; stir over heat, without boiling, until sugar dissolves. Bring to the boil; boil, uncovered, without stirring, until mixture is deep caramel in colour. Remove from heat; allow bubbles to subside. Pour toffee into deep 20cm (8 inch) round cake pan.
3 Combine cream and milk in medium saucepan; bring to the boil. Whisk eggs, extract and extra sugar in large bowl; whisking constantly, pour hot milk mixture into egg mixture. Strain mixture into cake pan.
4 Place pan in medium baking dish; add enough boiling water to come half way up side of pan. Bake about 40 minutes or until firm. Remove custard from baking dish, cover; refrigerate overnight.
5 Gently ease crème caramel from side of pan; invert onto deep-sided serving plate.

note **It's fine to use just 1 x 300ml carton of cream in this recipe.**

variations

vanilla bean **Add 1 split vanilla bean to cream and milk mixture before bringing to the boil; strain, remove vanilla bean before adding to egg mixture.**
cinnamon **Add 1 cinnamon stick to cream and milk mixture before bringing to the boil; strain, remove cinnamon stick before adding to egg mixture.**
orange **Stir 2 teaspoons finely grated orange rind into custard mixture before baking.**
hazelnut **Add 1 cup coarsely chopped roasted hazelnuts to cream and milk mixture; bring to the boil. Cover; stand 20 minutes then strain through muslin-lined sieve. Discard nuts. Bring cream and milk mixture back to the boil before whisking into egg mixture.**

SAUCES

HAZELNUT CREAM

prep time **20 minutes** makes **1 cup**

Beat $^2/_3$ cup pouring cream, 1 tablespoon
hazelnut-flavoured liqueur and 1 tablespoon
caster (superfine) sugar in small bowl with
electric mixer until soft peaks form; stir
$^1/_3$ cup coarsely chopped roasted hazelnuts
into cream.

note **We used Frangelico in this sauce, but the same
amounts of almond-flavoured liqueur and almonds
work just as well. Goes well with cold or warm cakes,
puddings and sweet crêpes.**

CRÈME ANGLAISE

prep & cook time **30 minutes**
(+ refrigeration) makes **1½ cups**

Split 1 vanilla bean in half lengthways; scrape
seeds into medium saucepan, add bean pod,
1½ cups milk and 1 tablespoon caster (superfine)
sugar. Bring to the boil then strain into large jug.
Discard pod. Combine 4 egg yolks and ¼ cup
caster sugar in medium heatproof bowl set over
medium saucepan of simmering water (do not
allow water to touch base of bowl). Whisk until
thick and creamy; gradually whisk in hot milk
mixture. Return custard mixture to pan; stir
over low heat until mixture is just thick enough
to coat the back of a spoon. Return custard
to bowl; refrigerate about 1 hour or until cold.

note **Goes well with poached plums, fresh figs, warm pies.**

BRANDY BUTTER

prep time **10 minutes (+ refrigeration)** makes **2 cups**

Beat 250g (8 ounces) softened unsalted
butter, ⅓ cup firmly packed light brown sugar,
1 teaspoon vanilla extract and ¼ cup brandy
in small bowl with electric mixer until light and
fluffy. Cover; refrigerate 1 hour.

notes **For a twist, try adding a little finely grated
orange rind or glacé ginger. Goes well with waffles
or crumpets, raisin toast, pancakes, fruit cake and
Christmas pudding.**

CHOCOLATE FUDGE SAUCE

prep & cook time **15 minutes** makes **1 cup**

Place 200g (6½ ounces) coarsely chopped
dark (semi-sweet) eating chocolate and 20g
(¾ ounce) butter in small heatproof bowl set
over small saucepan of simmering water (do
not allow water to touch base of bowl). Stir
until chocolate is melted. Add ¼ teaspoon
vanilla extract and ½ cup pouring cream; stir
until combined. Serve sauce warm.

note **Makes enough sauce for four servings of ice-cream.
Also goes well with puddings and poached fruit.**

LEMON CURD, BLUEBERRY AND MERINGUE TRIFLE

prep & cook time 50 minutes
(+ refrigeration and cooling) serves 6

2 cups (500ml) grape juice
90g (3 ounces) blueberry jelly crystals
200g (6½ ounces) sponge cake, cut into
    3cm pieces
¼ cup (60ml) sweet sherry
2 teaspoons finely grated lemon rind
¾ cup (180ml) lemon juice
1 cup (220g) caster (superfine) sugar
4 eggs
75g (2½ ounces) butter, chopped coarsely
1 teaspoon gelatine
1 tablespoon water
1¼ cups (310ml) thickened (heavy) cream
    (see notes)
45g (1½ ounces) meringue, chopped
    coarsely
2 cups (300g) fresh blueberries

1 Bring grape juice to the boil in small saucepan; stir in jelly crystals until dissolved. Pour jelly mixture into shallow container. Refrigerate about 20 minutes or until jelly is almost set.
2 Place cake in 3-litre (12-cup) bowl; sprinkle with sherry.
3 Combine rind, juice, sugar, eggs and butter in medium heatproof bowl. Place over medium saucepan of simmering water; cook, stirring, about 15 minutes or until curd coats the back of a spoon.
4 Sprinkle gelatine over the water in small heatproof jug. Stand jug in small saucepan of simmering water; stir until gelatine dissolves. Stir gelatine mixture into warm lemon curd. Cool to room temperature.
5 Pour jelly over cake; refrigerate 15 minutes. Top with lemon curd. Cover; refrigerate 3 hours or overnight.
6 Just before serving, beat cream in small bowl with electric mixer until soft peaks form; spread over curd. Sprinkle with meringue and berries.

notes It is fine just to use 1 x 300ml carton of cream for this recipe.
Although homemade lemon curd is divine, you can use store-bought lemon curd if you're short of time. Sponge cakes and meringues are also available, already prepared, from most supermarkets.

lime curd tart

LIME CURD TART

prep & cook time **45 minutes (+ refrigeration)** serves **10**

3 eggs
4 egg yolks
2 teaspoons finely grated lime rind
½ cup (125ml) lime juice
1 cup (220g) caster (superfine) sugar
200g (6½ ounces) unsalted butter, chopped
1 cup (50g) flaked coconut
pastry
1¼ cups (185g) plain (all-purpose) flour
½ cup (80g) icing (confectioners') sugar
¼ cup (20g) desiccated coconut
125g (4 ounces) cold unsalted butter
¼ cup (60ml) iced water, approximately

1 Make pastry.
2 Grease 24cm (9½ inch) round loose-based flan tin. Roll pastry between sheets of baking paper until large enough to line tin. Ease pastry into tin, press into base and side; trim edge, prick base with fork. Cover; refrigerate 30 minutes.
3 Preheat oven to 200°C/400°F.
4 Place tin on oven tray. Cover pastry case with baking paper, fill with dried beans or uncooked rice. Bake 15 minutes; remove paper and beans from pastry case. Bake about 10 minutes; cool.
5 Meanwhile, combine eggs, yolks, rind, juice, sugar and butter in medium saucepan; stir over medium heat, without boiling, about 15 minutes or until mixture coats the back of a spoon. Strain lime curd through sieve into medium bowl; stand 10 minutes then pour into pastry case. Refrigerate 2 hours before serving sprinkled with coconut.
pastry Process flour, sugar, coconut and butter until crumbly; add enough of the water to make ingredients come together. Knead dough gently on floured surface until smooth. Wrap in plastic wrap; refrigerate 30 minutes

white chocolate and black cherry creamed rice

WHITE CHOCOLATE AND BLACK CHERRY CREAMED RICE

prep & cook time **55 minutes** serves **6**

1.5 litres (6 cups) milk
⅔ cup (130g) arborio rice
2 tablespoons caster (superfine) sugar
90g (3 ounces) white eating chocolate, chopped finely
440g (14 ounces) canned seedless black cherries, drained

1 Combine milk, rice, sugar and half the chocolate in medium saucepan; bring to the boil. Reduce heat; cook over low heat, stirring often, about 40 minutes or until rice is tender.
2 Serve rice warm, topped with cherries and remaining chocolate. Serve sprinkled with nutmeg, if desired.

note **Arborio rice is a small, round-grain rice that is well-suited to absorb a large amount of liquid; it is especially suitable for risottos and creamed rice dishes, such as this one.**

crème brûlée

CRÈME BRÛLÉE

prep & cook time **55 minutes (+ refrigeration)** serves **6**

**1 vanilla bean
3 cups (750ml) thickened (heavy) cream
6 egg yolks
¼ cup (55g) caster (superfine) sugar
¼ cup (40g) pure icing (confectioners') sugar**

1 Preheat oven to 180°C/350°F. Grease six ½-cup (125ml) ovenproof dishes.
2 Split vanilla bean in half lengthways; scrape seeds into medium heatproof bowl. Heat pod with cream in small saucepan, without boiling.
3 Add egg yolks and caster sugar to seeds in bowl; gradually whisk in hot cream mixture. Set bowl over medium saucepan of simmering water; stir over heat about 10 minutes or until custard mixture thickens slightly and coats the back of a spoon; discard vanilla pod.
4 Place dishes in large baking dish; divide custard among dishes. Add enough boiling water to baking dish to come halfway up sides of ovenproof dishes. Bake about 20 minutes or until custard sets. Remove custards from dish; cool. Cover; refrigerate overnight.

5 Preheat grill. Place custards in shallow flameproof dish filled with ice cubes; sprinkle custards evenly with sifted icing sugar. Using finger, spread sugar over the surface of each custard, pressing in gently; grill until tops of crème brûlée caramelise.

PLUM CLAFOUTIS

prep & cook time **1 hour 10 minutes (+ cooling)** serves **6**

**10 small plums (750g), halved, seeded
1 cinnamon stick, halved
¼ cup (60ml) water
¼ cup (55g) light brown sugar
⅔ cup (160ml) milk
⅔ cup (160ml) pouring cream
1 teaspoon vanilla extract
4 eggs
½ cup (110g) caster (superfine) sugar
¼ cup (35g) plain (all-purpose) flour**

1 Preheat oven to 200°C/400°F. Grease shallow 2.5-litre (10-cup) ovenproof dish.
2 Place plums in medium baking dish with cinnamon and the water; sprinkle with brown sugar. Cook about 15 minutes or until plums have softened.
3 Remove cinnamon from dish and add to medium saucepan with milk, cream and extract; bring to the boil. Cool; remove cinnamon stick.
4 Whisk eggs and caster sugar in medium bowl until light and frothy; whisk in flour then whisk mixture into cream mixture.
5 Place drained plums in shallow ovenproof dish; pour cream mixture over plums. Bake about 30 minutes or until browned lightly. Serve dusted with icing (confectioners') sugar.

note **Use 1kg (2 pounds) canned whole plums if plums are not in season. Drain, halve and seed before using.**

plum clafoutis

CHOCOLATE TART

prep & cook time **1 hour 30 minutes**
(+ refrigeration) serves **8**

1½ cups (225g) plain (all-purpose) flour
½ cup (110g) caster (superfine) sugar
140g (4½ ounces) cold butter,
   chopped coarsely
1 egg
1 teaspoon cocoa powder
chocolate filling
2 eggs
2 egg yolks
¼ cup (55g) caster (superfine) sugar
250g (8 ounces) dark (semi-sweet) eating
   chocolate, melted
200g (6½ ounces) butter, melted

1 Process flour, sugar and butter until crumbly; add egg, process until ingredients come together. Knead dough on floured surface until smooth. Cover; refrigerate 30 minutes.
2 Roll pastry between sheets of baking paper until large enough to line greased 24cm (9½ inch) round loose-based flan tin. Lift pastry into tin; press into base and side, trim edge, prick base all over with fork. Cover; refrigerate 30 minutes.
3 Meanwhile, preheat oven to 200°C/400°F.
4 Make chocolate filling.
5 Place tin on oven tray. Cover pastry case with baking paper, fill with dried beans or rice. Bake 10 minutes. Remove paper and beans carefully from tin; bake about 5 minutes or until browned lightly. Cool.
6 Reduce oven temperature to 180°C/350°F.
7 Pour chocolate filling into pastry case. Bake about 10 minutes or until filling has set; cool 10 minutes. Refrigerate 1 hour. Serve dusted with sifted cocoa powder.
chocolate filling Whisk eggs, egg yolks and sugar in medium heatproof bowl over medium saucepan of simmering water (don't let water touch base of bowl) about 15 minutes or until light and fluffy. Gently whisk chocolate and butter into egg mixture.
Serve with **fresh berries of your choice.**

VERRINES (desserts in a glass)

BERRY COCONUT YOGURT PARFAITS

prep time **10 minutes** serves **6**

Blend or process 1 cup frozen mixed berries,
1 tablespoon caster (superfine) sugar, ¼ cup
raspberry and cranberry juice and 1 tablespoon
coconut-flavoured liqueur until smooth. Dip
12 sponge-finger biscuits in ¾ cup raspberry
and cranberry juice; divide among six 1½-cup
serving glasses. Divide 250g (8 ounces) vanilla
yogurt among glasses; top with half the berry
mixture. Repeat layering with another 250g
(8 ounces) vanilla yogurt and remaining berry
mixture. Sprinkle with 2 tablespoons toasted
flaked coconut.

note **Do not defrost berries before blending.**

RHUBARB FOOL

prep & cook time **30 minutes (+ refrigeration)** serves **4**

Combine 2 cups coarsely chopped rhubarb
in medium saucepan with ¼ cup caster
(superfine) sugar, ½ cup water and ½ teaspoon
ground cinnamon; bring to the boil. Reduce
heat; simmer, uncovered, stirring occasionally,
about 10 minutes or until rhubarb is tender.
Transfer to large bowl. Cover; refrigerate 1 hour.
Beat ¾ cup thickened (heavy) cream and
1 tablespoon icing (confectioners') sugar in
small bowl with electric mixer until soft peaks
form. Stir 1 cup prepared vanilla custard into
rhubarb mixture; fold whipped cream mixture
into rhubarb mixture. Divide fool among four
⅔ cup serving glasses. Refrigerate, covered,
for 1 hour before serving.

note **You need about four trimmed stalks of rhubarb for
this recipe.**

STRAWBERRIES ROMANOFF

prep time **10 minutes (+ refrigeration)** serves **4**

Combine 500g (1 pound) halved strawberries,
1½ tablespoons orange-flavoured liqueur and
2 teaspoons icing (confectioners') sugar in
large bowl; refrigerate 30 minutes. Drain
strawberries over small bowl; reserve liquid.
Divide three-quarters of the strawberries
among four serving dishes. Blend or process
remaining strawberries, 2 tablespoons icing
(confectioners') sugar and reserved liquid until
smooth. Beat ½ cup thickened (heavy) cream
in small bowl with electric mixer until soft peaks
form; fold in strawberry mixture. Top strawberries
with strawberry cream.

MELON TIRAMISU

prep time **30 minutes** serves **6**

Beat 1 cup thickened (heavy) cream and
1 tablespoon sifted icing (confectioners') sugar
in small bowl with electric mixer until soft peaks
form. Split 2 x 18cm (7 inch) round bought
sponge cakes in half horizontally; trim brown
edges. Cut 12 x 7cm (3 inch) rounds from
cakes. Place one cake round in each of six
1½ cup glasses; drizzle with 1½ tablespoons
melon-flavoured liqueur. Combine 300g
(9¾ ounces) coarsely chopped rockmelon
and 300g (9¾ ounces) coarsely chopped
honeydew melon in medium bowl. Divide half the
melons and cream over cake. Repeat layering
with remaining cake, another 1½ tablespoons
melon-flavoured liqueur and melon mixture.

note **We used Midori, a honeydew melon-flavoured
liqueur. This dessert is best made a day ahead and
refrigerated, covered, overnight.**

clove panna cotta with figs

CLOVE PANNA COTTA WITH FIGS

prep & cook time **30 minutes**
(+ cooling and refrigeration) serves **4**

1 teaspoon whole cloves
1¼ cups (310ml) thickened (heavy) cream
(see note)
⅔ cup (160ml) milk
2 teaspoons gelatine
2 tablespoons caster (superfine) sugar
½ teaspoon vanilla extract
2 tablespoons honey
4 medium fresh figs (240g), quartered

1 Grease four ½-cup (125ml) moulds.
2 Place cloves, cream and milk in small
saucepan; stand 10 minutes. Sprinkle gelatine
and sugar over cream mixture; stir over low
heat, without boiling, until gelatine and sugar
dissolve. Stir in extract. Strain into medium
jug; cool to room temperature.
3 Divide mixture among prepared moulds,
cover; refrigerate 3 hours or until set.
4 Stir honey in small saucepan until warm.
5 Turn panna cotta onto serving plates; serve
with figs drizzled with honey.

note **It's fine to use just 1 x 300ml carton of cream.**

BERRY FRANGIPANE TART

prep & cook time **50 minutes** serves **6**

1 sheet ready-rolled sweet puff pastry
300g (9¾ ounces) frozen mixed berries
frangipane
75g (2½ ounces) butter, softened
½ teaspoon vanilla extract
⅓ cup (75g) caster (superfine) sugar
2 egg yolks
1 tablespoon plain (all-purpose) flour
1 cup (120g) ground almonds

1 Preheat oven to 220°C/425°F. Grease
20cm x 30cm (8 inch x 12 inch) lamington pan.
2 Roll pastry until large enough to cover base
and sides of pan; line pan with pastry, press
into sides. Prick pastry all over with fork; freeze
5 minutes.
3 Place another lamington pan on top of pastry;
bake 5 minutes. Remove top pan; bake about
5 minutes or until pastry is browned lightly. Cool
5 minutes. Reduce temperature to 180°C/350°F.
4 Meanwhile, make frangipane.
5 Spread frangipane over pastry base. Sprinkle
with berries, press into frangipane. Bake about
30 minutes or until browned lightly.
frangipane Beat butter, extract, sugar and
egg yolks in small bowl with electric mixer until
light and fluffy. Stir in flour and ground almonds.

note **Frangipane is a delicious almond-flavoured filling
for pies, tarts and cakes. We've used mixed berries in
this recipe, however, you can use any berries you like. It
is important to use frozen berries to prevent the colour
bleeding dramatically through the frangipane as it cooks.**

berry frangipane tart

frozen peanut butter cheesecake

FROZEN PEANUT BUTTER CHEESECAKE

prep & cook time **40 minutes**
(+ cooling and freezing) serves **16**

250g (8 ounces) chocolate chip biscuits
45g (1½ ounces) butter, melted
1 tablespoon milk
peanut butter filling
¾ cup (210g) crunchy peanut butter
½ cup (125ml) pouring cream
250g (8 ounces) cream cheese, softened
½ cup (110g) caster (superfine) sugar
hot chocolate sauce
200g (6½ ounces) dark (semi-sweet) eating
    chocolate, chopped coarsely
20g (¾ ounce) butter
½ cup (125ml) pouring cream

1 Grease 24cm (9½ inch) round loose-based flan tin.
2 Process biscuits until fine; add butter and milk, process until combined. Press mixture over base and side of tin. Freeze 30 minutes.
3 Make peanut butter filling. Spread filling over crust; cover with foil, freeze 3 hours or overnight.
4 Make hot chocolate sauce; serve with cheesecake.
peanut butter filling Combine peanut butter and cream in small saucepan; stir over low heat until smooth. Cool 15 minutes. Beat cream cheese and sugar in small bowl with electric mixer until smooth. Stir in peanut butter mixture.
hot chocolate sauce Combine ingredients in small saucepan; stir over low heat until smooth.

BAKLAVA CHEESECAKE

prep & cook time **35 minutes (+ refrigeration)** serves **16**

⅓ cup (35g) walnuts
⅔ cup (90g) pistachios
2 teaspoons mixed spice
250g (8 ounces) butternut snap cookies
½ cup (70g) slivered almonds
125g (4 ounces) unsalted butter, melted
cheesecake filling
3 teaspoons gelatine
¼ cup (60ml) water

baklava cheesecake

500g (1 pound) cream cheese, softened
½ cup (110g) caster (superfine) sugar
¼ cup (90g) honey
1½ cups (375ml) thickened (heavy) cream

1 Preheat oven to 220°C/425°F. Grease 26cm (10½ inch) springform tin.
2 Roast walnuts and pistachios on oven tray about 5 minutes. Sprinkle nuts with spice; roast 1 minute, cool. Process nuts with cookies until chopped finely; transfer to medium bowl, stir in almonds.
3 Set aside one-third of the nut mixture. Stir butter into remaining nut mixture. Press mixture evenly over base of tin; refrigerate 30 minutes.
4 Meanwhile, make cheesecake filling.
5 Pour filling into tin; sprinkle top with reserved nut mixture. Cover; refrigerate overnight.
cheesecake filling Sprinkle gelatine over the water in small heatproof jug; stand jug in small saucepan of simmering water. Stir until gelatine dissolves; cool 5 minutes. Beat cream cheese, sugar and honey in medium bowl with electric mixer until smooth; beat in cream, then stir in gelatine mixture.

HAZELNUT PRALINE TIRAMISU

prep & cook time 50 minutes
(+ standing and refrigeration) serves 15

¼ cup (30g) ground coffee
2 cups (500ml) boiling water
1 cup (250ml) marsala
4 egg yolks
¼ cup (55g) caster (superfine) sugar
1kg (4 cups) mascarpone cheese
¼ cup (60ml) marsala, extra
½ cup (110g) caster (superfine) sugar, extra
500g (1 pound) sponge finger biscuits
100g (3½ pounds) coarsely grated dark
   (semi-sweet) eating chocolate
hazelnut praline
¼ cup (35g) hazelnuts
⅓ cup (75g) caster (superfine) sugar
2 tablespoons water

1 Using coffee and the boiling water, prepare coffee in a plunger. Stand for 2 minutes, plunge coffee; pour into large jug, stir in liqueur.
2 Beat egg yolks and sugar in small bowl with electric mixer until thick and creamy.
3 Beat mascarpone, extra liqueur and extra sugar in large bowl with electric mixer until slightly thickened. Gently fold in egg yolk mixture.

4 Pour half the coffee mixture into shallow bowl. Dip half the biscuits, a couple at a time, into coffee mixture until beginning to soften. Line base of 3-litre (12-cup) serving dish with biscuits; brush with any unused coffee mixture. Spread biscuits with half the mascarpone mixture and sprinkle with half the grated chocolate. Repeat with remaining biscuits, coffee mixture and mascarpone. Cover; refrigerate overnight.
5 Make hazelnut praline.
6 Just before serving, sprinkle with remaining chocolate and hazelnut praline.
hazelnut praline Preheat oven to 180°C/350°F. Place hazelnuts in shallow baking dish; bake about 8 minutes or until skins split. Rub nuts in tea towel to remove most of the skin; cool. Grease oven tray. Combine sugar and the water in small saucepan; stir over low heat until sugar dissolves. Brush side of pan with pastry brush dipped in water to remove sugar crystals. Bring to the boil. Boil, uncovered, without stirring, about 5 minutes or until mixture turns a toffee colour. Remove from heat, stir in nuts then quickly pour onto prepared tray. Stand at room temperature until set. Blend or process praline until roughly chopped.

notes Tiramisu is best prepared a day ahead. Hazelnut praline can be made several days ahead; store in an airtight container.

FROZEN MOCHA MOUSSE

prep time 1 hour (+ freezing and refrigeration) serves 10

dark chocolate layer
100g (3½ ounces) dark (semi-sweet)
    eating chocolate, melted
2 teaspoons coffee-flavoured liqueur
2 eggs, separated
½ cup (125ml) thickened (heavy) cream

milk chocolate layer
100g (3½ ounces) milk eating chocolate, melted
2 tablespoons coffee-flavoured liqueur
2 eggs, separated
½ cup (125ml) thickened (heavy) cream

white chocolate layer
125g (4 ounces) white eating chocolate, melted
60g (2 ounces) butter, melted
2 teaspoons coffee-flavoured liqueur
3 eggs, separated
⅔ cup (160ml) thickened (heavy) cream

nutty chocolate sauce
½ cup (165g) hazelnut spread
¾ cup (180ml) thickened (heavy) cream
1 tablespoon coffee-flavoured liqueur

1 Line 14cm x 21cm (5½ inch x 8½ inch)
loaf pan with plastic wrap.
2 To make dark chocolate layer, combine
chocolate, liqueur and egg yolks in large bowl;
stir until smooth. Beat cream in small bowl with
electric mixer until soft peaks form; fold into
chocolate mixture. Beat egg whites in small
bowl with electric mixer until soft peaks form;
fold into chocolate mixture.
3 Pour dark chocolate mixture into prepared
pan; cover with foil, freeze until firm.

4 Make milk chocolate layer; pour over dark
chocolate layer. Cover; freeze until firm.
5 Make white chocolate layer; pour over milk
chocolate layer. Cover; freeze until firm.
6 Make nutty chocolate sauce.
7 Turn mousse onto serving plate; remove
plastic wrap. Slice mousse, serve with nutty
chocolate sauce.

milk chocolate layer Combine chocolate,
liqueur and egg yolks in large bowl; stir until
smooth. Beat cream in small bowl with electric
mixer until soft peaks form; fold into chocolate
mixture. Beat egg whites in small bowl with
electric mixer until soft peaks form; fold into
chocolate mixture.

white chocolate layer Combine chocolate,
butter, liqueur and egg yolks in large bowl; stir
until smooth. Beat cream in small bowl with
electric mixer until soft peaks form; fold into
chocolate mixture. Beat egg whites in small
bowl with electric mixer until soft peaks form;
fold into chocolate mixture.

nutty chocolate sauce Place hazelnut spread
in small heatproof bowl; stir over small saucepan
of simmering water until pourable. Gradually
stir in cream and liqueur; refrigerate until cool.

notes The mousse can be made up to a week ahead;
keep, covered, in the freezer.
Any coffee-flavoured liqueur, such as Kahlua or
Tia Maria, can be used.

LEMON TART

prep & cook time **1 hour 25 minutes**
(+ refrigeration) serves **8**

1¼ cups (185g) plain (all-purpose) flour
⅓ cup (55g) icing (confectioners') sugar
¼ cup (30g) ground almonds
125g (4 ounces) cold butter, chopped
1 egg yolk
2 tablespoons iced water
lemon filling
3 teaspoons finely grated lemon rind
⅓ cup (80ml) lemon juice
3 eggs
½ cup (110g) caster (superfine) sugar
⅔ cup (160ml) pouring cream

1 Blend or process flour, icing sugar, ground almonds and butter until crumbly. Add egg yolk and the water; process until combined. Knead dough on floured surface until smooth. Wrap in plastic wrap; refrigerate 30 minutes.
2 Roll pastry between sheets of baking paper until large enough to line 24cm (9½ inch) round loose-based flan tin. Lift pastry into tin; press into side, trim edge. Cover; refrigerate 30 minutes.

3 Meanwhile, preheat oven to 200°C/400°F.
4 Place tin on oven tray. Line pastry case with baking paper, fill with dried beans or rice. Bake 15 minutes. Remove paper and beans; bake about 10 minutes or until browned lightly.
5 Meanwhile, whisk ingredients for lemon filling in medium bowl; stand 5 minutes.
6 Reduce oven temperature to 180°C/350°F.
7 Pour lemon filling into pastry case; bake about 30 minutes or until filling has set slightly, cool.
8 Refrigerate until cold. Serve dusted with sifted icing sugar, if desired.
Serve with **whipped cream; dust tart with sifted icing sugar just before serving.**

notes **This tart is best made a day ahead; keep, covered, in the refrigerator. You will need about three lemons for the filling.**

ICE-CREAM

ICE-CREAM SELECTION

prep time **5 minutes** serves **4**

Buy and freeze a variety of individual tub
servings of the best quality ice-cream you
can find. Pile all the ice-cream tubs onto a large
serving bowl or tray, and take it to the table for
guests to choose their own. Don't forget the tiny
spoons. Or, simply buy the best quality gelato in
whatever flavour you think suits the rest of the
meal; when in doubt, buy lemon-flavoured
gelato, it's probably the most popular of all.

COFFEE HAZELNUT SHOTS

prep & cook time **20 minutes** serves **4**

Combine ⅓ cup hazelnut-flavoured liqueur,
¼ cup water, 2 tablespoons instant coffee
granules and 2 tablespoons light brown sugar
in small saucepan; stir over low heat until sugar
dissolves. Boil about 5 minutes or until syrup
thickens slightly. Divide 2 cups hazelnut gelato
among four serving glasses; pour over coffee
syrup. Serve sprinkled with ¼ cup coarsely
chopped roasted hazelnuts.

BANANA CARAMEL SUNDAE

prep & cook time **20 minutes** serves **6**

To make caramel sauce, combine 100g
(3½ ounces) butter, ½ cup pouring cream
and ½ cup firmly packed light brown sugar
in small saucepan. Stir over low heat until
sugar dissolves; bring to the boil. Reduce
heat; simmer, uncovered, 5 minutes. Cool.
Layer caramel sauce, 75g (2½ ounces) finely
chopped dark (semi-sweet) eating chocolate,
²/₃ cup coarsely chopped roasted walnuts,
1 litre (4 cups) vanilla ice-cream and 4 coarsely
chopped medium bananas in six ¾-cup
(180ml) glasses.

BLACK FOREST ICE-CREAM SANDWICH

prep & cook time **25 minutes** serves **4**

Drain 410g (13 ounces) canned seedless
cherries in syrup; reserve cherries and syrup
separately. Stir syrup and ¼ cup caster
(superfine) sugar in small saucepan over heat
until sugar dissolves. Boil, uncovered, about
5 minutes or until syrup thickens slightly.
Meanwhile, halve 4 x 6cm (2¼ inch) square
lamingtons. Sandwich 4 x 45g (1½ ounce)
vanilla ice-cream slices between lamingtons.
Place onto serving plates; top with cherries
then drizzle with syrup.

note **You can trim the ice-cream slice to fit the lamington.**

SUMMER PUDDING

prep & cook time **55 minutes (+ refrigeration)** serves **6**

3 eggs
½ cup (110g) caster (superfine) sugar
1 tablespoon cornflour (cornstarch)
¾ cup (110g) self-raising flour
1 teaspoon butter
¼ cup (60ml) boiling water
⅓ cup (75g) caster (superfine) sugar, extra
½ cup (125ml) water
2 cups (300g) frozen blackberries
3⅓ cups (500g) frozen mixed berries
¼ cup (80g) blackberry jam

1 Preheat oven to 180°C/350°F. Grease 25cm x 30cm (10 inch x 12 inch) swiss roll pan; line base with baking paper, extending paper 5cm (2 inches) over long sides.
2 Beat eggs in small bowl with electric mixer until thick and creamy. Gradually add sugar, beating until sugar dissolves; transfer mixture to large bowl.
3 Fold triple-sifted flours into egg mixture. Pour combined butter and boiling water down side of bowl; fold into egg mixture. Spread mixture into pan; bake about 15 minutes. Cool in pan.

4 Meanwhile, combine extra sugar and the water in medium saucepan; bring to the boil. Stir in berries; return to the boil. Reduce heat; simmer, uncovered, until berries soften. Strain over medium bowl; reserve syrup and berries separately.
5 Turn cake onto board. Line 1.25-litre (5-cup) pudding basin with plastic wrap, extending wrap 10cm (4 inches) over side of basin. Cut circle slightly smaller than top edge of basin from cake using tip of sharp knife; cut second circle exact size of base of basin from cake. Cut remaining cake into 10cm (4 inch) long strips.
6 Place small cake circle in bottom of basin and use cake strips to line side of basin. Pour ⅔ cup of the reserved syrup into small jug; reserve. Fill basin with berries; cover with remaining syrup, top with large cake circle. Cover pudding with overhanging plastic wrap, weight pudding with saucer; refrigerate 3 hours or overnight.
7 Stir jam and two tablespoons of the reserved syrup in small saucepan until heated through. Turn pudding onto serving plate; brush with remaining reserved syrup then jam mixture. Serve with whipped cream, if you like.

BAKED CHEESECAKE WITH LIQUEUR CHERRIES

prep & cook time **1 hour 35 minutes**
(+ refrigeration and cooling) serves **12**

**180g (6 ounces) plain sweet biscuits
(see notes)**
125g (4 ounces) butter, melted
500g (1 pound) cream cheese, softened
**250g (8 ounces) mascarpone cheese,
softened**
1 cup (220g) caster (superfine) sugar
2 teaspoons finely grated lemon rind
2 teaspoons vanilla extract
3 eggs
liqueur cherries
300g (9¾ ounces) frozen cherries
2 tablespoons kirsch
1 tablespoon water
1 tablespoon caster (superfine) sugar
1 teaspoon lemon juice

1 Grease 24cm (9½ inch) springform tin; line
side with baking paper.
2 Blend or process biscuits until fine. Add butter;
blend until combined. Press mixture over base of
tin; place tin on oven tray, refrigerate 30 minutes.
3 Preheat oven to 200°C/400°F.
4 Bake biscuit crust 10 minutes; cool.
5 Reduce oven temperature to 180°C/350°F.
6 Beat cream cheese, mascarpone, sugar, rind
and extract in medium bowl with electric mixer
until smooth. Beat in eggs, one at a time. Do
not overbeat.
7 Pour filling into crust; bake 50 minutes. Cool
cheesecake in oven with door ajar. Cover;
refrigerate 3 hours or overnight.
8 Make liqueur cherries. Top cheesecake with
liqueur cherries before serving.
liqueur cherries Combine ingredients in
medium saucepan; bring to the boil. Reduce
heat; simmer about 10 minutes or until mixture
is slightly thickened.

notes **Kirch is a cherry-flavoured liqueur.**
**We used a mixture of 90g (3 ounces) shredded wheatmeal
biscuits and 90g (3 ounces) morning coffee biscuits for
the crust. Any plain sweet biscuits (cookies) will be fine.**

FAST FRUIT DESSERTS

GRILLED PINEAPPLE WITH COCONUT ICE-CREAM

prep & cook time **25 minutes (+ freezing)** serves **4**

Fold 1 cup toasted shredded coconut and ¼ cup coconut-flavoured liqueur into 1 litre (4 cups) softened vanilla ice-cream; freeze, covered, overnight. Combine 1 tablespoon coconut-flavoured liqueur and 2 tablespoons light brown sugar in large bowl; add 1 thickly sliced large pineapple, toss to coat in sugar mixture. Cook pineapple on heated oiled grill plate (or grill or barbecue) until browned both sides; serve with coconut ice-cream.

PEACH MELBA

prep & cook time **10 minutes (+ cooling)** serves **4**

Place 1 litre (4 cups) water in medium saucepan; bring to the boil. Add 4 medium peaches; simmer, uncovered, 5 minutes. Remove peaches; place in bowl of cold water. When peaches are cold, remove skins. Meanwhile, push 200g (6½ ounces) fresh or thawed frozen raspberries through fine sieve into small bowl; sweeten pulp with 1 tablespoon sifted icing (confectioners') sugar to taste. Serve peach halves topped with 2 cups (500ml) vanilla ice-cream, raspberry sauce and extra raspberries.

STRAWBERRIES AND MINT IN ORANGE SYRUP

prep & cook time **15 minutes (+ cooling)** serves **4**

Stir ¼ cup water and 2 tablespoons grated palm sugar in small saucepan, over low heat, until sugar dissolves; bring to the boil. Boil, uncovered, without stirring, about 3 minutes or until syrup thickens slightly. Remove from heat; stir in 2 teaspoons finely grated orange rind and 2 tablespoons orange juice; cool. Combine 500g (1 pound) quartered strawberries and ¼ cup coarsely chopped fresh mint in medium bowl with syrup. Divide mixture into bowls; serve with ⅔ cup crème fraîche.

CHOCOLATY BANANAS

prep & cook time **35 minutes** serves **4**

Cut 12cm (4¾ inch) long slit into 4 unpeeled bananas; place bananas on pieces of foil. Chop 155g (5 ounces) dark (semi-sweet) eating chocolate coarsely; divide among cuts. Drizzle 2 tablespoons rum into cuts; wrap bananas in foil. Cook on heated grill plate (or grill or barbecue) about 30 minutes or until skins blacken. Serve with whipped cream.

TROPICAL FRUIT WITH ORANGE GLAZE

prep & cook time **20 minutes** serves **4**

To make orange glaze, combine 1 teaspoon finely grated orange rind, 2 tablespoons orange juice and 2 tablespoons light brown sugar in small saucepan; stir over low heat until sugar dissolves. Cool. Preheat grill (broiler). Combine glaze with 1 trimmed, halved and thickly sliced small pineapple, 2 quartered medium bananas and 1 thickly sliced starfruit in large bowl. Spread fruit mixture onto two foil-lined oven trays. Grill fruit about 5 minutes or until browned lightly. Serve fruit sprinkled with ¼ cup loosely packed fresh mint leaves.

CARAMELISED PEACHES

prep & cook time **15 minutes** serves **4**

Combine 1 cup yogurt with ¼ teaspoon ground cinnamon and ¼ teaspoon ground cardamom in bowl. Halve 4 peaches. Cook peach halves, cut-side down, on heated oiled grill plate (or grill or barbecue) until browned. Sprinkle 2 tablespoons light brown sugar over cut sides; cook, cut-sides down, until sugar bubbles. Serve peaches with spiced yogurt.

SUMMER FRUIT SALAD WITH MINTED SUGAR

prep time **15 minutes** serves **4**

Blend or process ¼ cup loosely packed fresh mint leaves, 2 tablespoons white sugar and 2 teaspoons finely grated lemon rind until chopped finely. Combine 2 cored and thinly sliced medium pears, 155g (5 ounces) blackberries, 125g (4 ounces) halved strawberries and 100g (3½ ounces) halved seedless green grapes in medium bowl. Serve fruit salad with minted sugar.

CHERRIES JUBILEE

prep & cook time **15 minutes** serves **4**

Drain 410g (13 ounces) canned seeded black cherries; reserve cherries and syrup, separately. Combine syrup, 1 tablespoon caster (superfine) sugar and 1 cinnamon stick in small saucepan; cook, stirring, until mixture boils. Reduce heat; simmer, uncovered, without stirring, 2 minutes. Strain syrup into small heatproof bowl; discard cinnamon. Return syrup to pan; stir in blended 2 teaspoons arrowroot and 1 tablespoon water. Cook, stirring, until mixture boils and thickens slightly. Add cherries; stir until heated through. Heat ⅓ cup brandy in small saucepan; stir into cherry mixture. Serve immediately with whipped cream and macaroons.

GLOSSARY

ALLSPICE also known as pimento or jamaican pepper; so-named because is tastes like a combination of nutmeg, cumin, clove and cinnamon – all spices.

ALMONDS flat, pointy-ended nuts with pitted brown shell enclosing a creamy white kernel that is covered by a brown skin.

blanched nuts with skins removed.

flaked paper-thin slices.

ground also known as almond meal; nuts are powdered to a coarse flour-like texture.

slivered flat lengthways-cut pieces.

BAKING PAPER also known as parchment paper or baking parchment; a silicone-coated paper primarily used for lining baking pans and oven trays so cakes and biscuits won't stick, making for removal easy.

BICARBONATE OF SODA also known as baking or carb soda.

BUTTER use salted or unsalted (sweet) butter; 125g is equal to one stick (4 ounces) of butter.

unsalted butter, often called "sweet" butter, simply has no added salt. It is mainly used in baking, and if the recipe calls for unsalted butter, then it should not be substituted.

CARAMEL TOP 'N' FILL a caramel filling made from milk and cane sugar. Can be used straight from the can for tarts, cheesecakes and slices. Has similar qualities to sweetened condensed milk, only a thicker, caramel consistency.

CHOCOLATE

choc Bits also known as chocolate chips and chocolate morsels. Made of cocoa liquor, cocoa butter, sugar and an emulsifier; these hold their shape in baking.

chocolate Melts are discs of compounded dark chocolate ideal for melting and moulding.

dark eating also known as semi-sweet or luxury chocolate; made of a high percentage of cocoa liquor and cocoa butter, and a little added sugar. Unless stated otherwise, we use dark eating chocolate in this book.

milk the most popular eating chocolate, mild and very sweet; similar in make-up to dark with the difference being the addition of milk solids.

chocolate-hazelnut spread we use Nutella. Originally developed when chocolate was in short supply during World War 2, so hazelnuts were added to increase supply.

white eating contains no cocoa solids but derives its sweet flavour from cocoa butter. Is very sensitive to heat.

CINNAMON dried inner bark of the shoots of the cinnamon tree; available in stick (quill) or ground form.

CLOVES dried flower buds of a tropical tree; can be used whole or in ground form. Has a distinctively pungent and "spicy" scent and flavour.

COCOA POWDER also known as cocoa; dried, unsweetened, roasted then ground cocoa beans (cacao seeds).

COCONUT

desiccated unsweetened, concentrated, dried, finely shredded coconut.

flaked dried, flaked, coconut flesh.

shredded long thin strips of dried coconut.

CORN FLAKES commercially manufactured cereal made of dehydrated then baked crisp flakes of corn.

CORNFLOUR also known as cornstarch; used as a thickening agent. Available as 100% corn (maize) and wheaten cornflour.

CORN SYRUP a thick, sweet syrup created by processing cornstarch; comes in light or dark forms. Light corn syrup has been clarified to remove all colour and cloudiness; dark corn syrup, which has caramel flavour and colouring added to it, has a deeper colour and stronger flavour.

CRANBERRIES, DRIED they have the same slightly sour, succulent flavour as fresh cranberries. Available in most supermarkets.

CREAM we used fresh cream, unless otherwise stated. Also known as pure cream and pouring cream; has no additives unlike commercially thickened cream. Minimum fat content 35%.

thickened a whipping cream with 35% minimum fat content.

CREAM CHEESE commonly known as Philadelphia or Philly, a soft cows'-milk cheese with a fat content of at least 33%.

CREAM OF TARTAR the acid ingredient in baking powder; added to confectionery mixtures to help prevent sugar from crystallising. Keeps frostings creamy and improves volume when beating egg whites.

CURRANTS dried tiny, almost black raisins so-named after a grape variety that originated in Corinth, Greece.

CUSTARD POWDER instant mixture used to make pouring custard; similar to North American instant pudding mixes.

DATES fruit of the date palm tree, eaten fresh or dried, on their own or in prepared dishes. About 4cm to 6cm in length, oval and plump, thin-skinned, with a honey-sweet flavour and sticky texture.

FLOUR
  plain an all-purpose flour made from wheat.
  rice a very fine flour made from ground white rice.
  self-raising plain flour sifted with baking powder in the proportion of 1 cup flour to 2 teaspoons baking powder.
  wholemeal flour milled from whole wheat grain (bran, germ and endosperm). Available as plain or self-raising.

FOOD COLOURING dyes that can be used to change the colour of various foods.

GELATINE three teaspoons of powdered gelatine (8g or one sachet) is roughly equivalent to four gelatine leaves.

GINGER, GROUND also known as powdered ginger; cannot be substituted for fresh ginger.

glacé ginger is made from fresh ginger root preserved in sugar syrup. Crystallised ginger can be substituted if rinsed with warm water then dried.

GLACÉ CHERRIES also called candied cherries; these are boiled in a heavy sugar syrup, then dried. Found in health food stores and supermarkets.

GLACÉ ORANGES are slices of orange preserved in a sugar syrup. Found in health food stores and some of the larger supermarkets.

GOLDEN SYRUP a by-product of refined sugarcane; honey can be substituted.

HAZELNUTS also known as filberts; plump, grape-size, rich, sweet nut having a brown inedible skin that is removed by rubbing heated nuts together vigorously in a tea towel.
  hazelnuts, ground have been ground into a course or fine powder. Also known as hazelnut meal.

JAM also known as preserve or conserve; most often made from fruit.

JERSEY CARAMELS two layers of sweet condensed milk caramel sandwiching a layer of white caramel. Soft, chewy and sweet.

LAMINGTON PAN a 20cm x 30cm x 3cm (12" x 8" x 1") slab cake pan.

MALTED MILK POWDER a combination of wheat flour, malt flour and milk, which are evaporated to give the powder its fine appearance and to make it easily absorbable in liquids.

MANDARIN small, loose-skinned citrus fruit that is also known as tangerine.

MARMALADE a preserve, usually based on citrus fruit.

MARZIPAN an almond and sugar paste used to ice cakes and other pastries or sculpted into a variety of shapes to be eaten as candy or used as decorations.

MILK
  full-cream milk powder an evaporated pasteurised milk concentrate, containing about 40% milk solids, is dried to reduce the moisture content to about 3% and prevent particles from clumping together.
  sweetened condensed milk has had 60% of the water removed; the remaining milk is then sweetened with sugar.

MIXED DRIED FRUIT combination of sultanas, raisins, currants, mixed peel and cherries.

MIXED SPICE a blend of ground spices – usually cinnamon, allspice and nutmeg.

NUTMEG the dried nut of an evergreen tree native to Indonesia; it is available in ground form or you can grate your own with a fine grater.

OATS
  quick cooking oats are generally thinner than rolled oats, so absorb more water and cook faster; they are thicker than "instant" oats.
  rolled oats are oat groats (oats that have been husked) steamed-softened, flattened with rollers, dried and then packaged for consumption as a cereal product.

ORANGE BLOSSOM WATER also known as orange flower water; a concentrated flavouring made from orange blossoms. Available from Middle-Eastern food stores and some major supermarkets and delis. Can not be substituted with citrus flavourings as the taste is completely different.

PASSIONFRUIT also known as granadilla; a small tropical fruit, native to Brazil, comprised of a tough outer skin surrounding edible black sweet-sour seeds. Six large passionfruit give about ½ cup of pulp.

PASTRY
  ready-rolled puff packaged sheets of frozen puff pastry, available from supermarkets.
  ready-rolled shortcrust packaged sheets of shortcrust pastry (sweet or savoury), available from supermarkets.

PEANUT BUTTER peanuts are ground to a paste; available in crunchy and smooth varieties.

PEANUTS not, in fact, a nut but the pod of a legume.

PECANS native to the United States and now grown locally; a golden-brown, rich buttery nut.

PISTACHIO pale green, delicately flavoured nut inside hard off-white shells. To peel, soak shelled nuts in boiling water for about 5 minutes; drain, then pat dry with absorbent paper. Rub skins with a cloth to peel.

POLENTA also known as cornmeal; a flour-like cereal made of dried corn (maize) sold ground in different textures (from fine to coarse).

PUMPKIN SEED KERNELS also known as pepitas.

ROLLED OATS, see oats.

ROSEWATER distilled from rose petals; used in the Middle East, North Africa and India to flavour desserts. Don't confuse this with rose essence, which is more concentrated.

SUGAR
  caster also known as superfine or finely granulated table sugar.
  dark brown a moist, dark brown sugar with a rich distinctive full flavour coming from natural molasses syrup.
  demerara small-grained golden-coloured crystal sugar.
  light brown an extremely soft, finely granulated sugar retaining molasses for its characteristic colour and flavour.
  icing sugar also known as confectioners' sugar or powdered sugar; granulated sugar crushed together with a small amount of cornflour.
  icing sugar, pure also known as confectioners' sugar or powdered sugar, but has no added cornflour.
  white a coarse, granulated table sugar, also known as crystal sugar.

SULTANAS dried grapes, also known as golden raisins.

SUNFLOWER SEED KERNELS sunflower kernels from dried husked sunflower seeds.

SWEETENED CONDENSED MILK, see milk.

TREACLE a concentrated sugar syrup with a distinctive flavour and dark black colour.

VANILLA
  beans dried long, thin pod from a tropical golden orchid grown in Central and South America and Tahiti; the minuscule black seeds inside the bean are used to impart a luscious vanilla flavour in baking and desserts. Beans can be added to caster sugar to give it a lovely vanilla flavour.
  extract made by pulping chopped vanilla beans with a mixture of alcohol and water. This gives a very strong solution, and only a couple of drops are needed to flavour most dishes.
  paste made from vanilla bean extract, vanilla bean seeds, sugar and natural thickeners. Can be used as a substitute for vanilla bean.

VEGETABLE OIL sourced from plants rather than animals.

WALNUTS the fruit of the walnut tree, which grows in temperate zones throughout the world; is rich and flavourful. Should be stored in the refrigerator because of its high oil content.

WHEAT GERM is where the seed germinates to form the sprout that becomes wheat. The term "germ" comes from the word germinate. It has a nutty flavour and is very oily, which causes it to turn rancid quickly. Wheat germ is usually separated from the bran and starch during the milling of flour because its perishable oil content limits the keeping time of the flour. It is available from health-food stores and supermarkets.

CONVERSION CHART

MEASURES

One Australian metric measuring cup holds approximately 250ml, one Australian metric tablespoon holds 20ml, one Australian metric teaspoon holds 5ml.

The difference between one country's measuring cups and another's is within a 2- or 3-teaspoon variance, and will not affect your cooking results. North America, New Zealand and the United Kingdom use a 15ml tablespoon. All cup and spoon measurements are level. The most accurate way of measuring dry ingredients is to weigh them. When measuring liquids, use a clear glass or plastic jug with metric markings.

We use large eggs with an average weight of 60g.

DRY MEASURES

METRIC	IMPERIAL
15g	½oz
30g	1oz
60g	2oz
90g	3oz
125g	4oz (¼lb)
155g	5oz
185g	6oz
220g	7oz
250g	8oz (½lb)
280g	9oz
315g	10oz
345g	11oz
375g	12oz (¾lb)
410g	13oz
440g	14oz
470g	15oz
500g	16oz (1lb)
750g	24oz (1½lb)
1kg	32oz (2lb)

LIQUID MEASURES

METRIC	IMPERIAL
30ml	1 fluid oz
60mi	2 fluid oz
100ml	3 fluid oz
125ml	4 fluid oz
150ml	5 fluid oz
190ml	6 fluid oz
250ml	8 fluid oz
300ml	10 fluid oz
500ml	16 fluid oz
600ml	20 fluid oz
1000ml (1 litre)	1¾ pints

LENGTH MEASURES

METRIC	IMPERIAL
3mm	⅛in
6mm	¼in
1cm	½in
2cm	¾in
2.5cm	1in
5cm	2in
6cm	2½in
8cm	3in
10cm	4in
13cm	5in
15cm	6in
18cm	7in
20cm	8in
23cm	9in
25cm	10in
28cm	11in
30cm	12in (1ft)

OVEN TEMPERATURES

These oven temperatures are only a guide for conventional ovens. For fan-forced ovens, check the manufacturer's manual.

	°C (CELSIUS)	°F (FAHRENHEIT)
Very slow	120	250
Slow	150	275-300
Moderately slow	160	325
Moderate	180	350-375
Moderately hot	200	400
Hot	220	425-450
Very hot	240	475

Measurements for cake pans are approximate only. Using same-shaped cake pans of a similar size should not affect the outcome of your baking. We measure the inside top of the cake pan to determine sizes.

INDEX

First Published in 2010 by ACP Magazines Ltd,

a division of PBL Media Pty Limited

54 Park St, Sydney

GPO Box 4088, Sydney, NSW 2001.

phone (02) 9282 8618; fax (02) 9267 9438

acpbooks@acpmagazines.com.au; www.acpbooks.com.au

ACP BOOKS

General Manager - Christine Whiston

Editor-in-Chief - Susan Tomnay

Creative Director & Designer - Hieu Chi Nguyen

Food Director - Pamela Clark

Published and Distributed in the United Kingdom by Octopus Publishing Group

Endeavour House

189 Shaftesbury Avenue

London WC2H 8JY

United Kingdom

phone (+44)(0)207 632 5400; fax (+44)(0)207 632 5405

info@octopus-publishing.co.uk;

www.octopusbooks.co.uk

Printed by Toppan Printing Co., China

International foreign language rights, Brian Cearnes, ACP Books bcearnes@acpmagazines.com.au

A catalogue record for this book is available from the British Library.

ISBN : 978 1 86396 9338 (pbk.)